Everyone Feels
ANGRY
Sometimes

by Cari Meister
illustrated by Damian Ward

PICTURE WINDOW BOOKS
a capstone imprint

Thanks to our adviser for his expertise:

Terry Flaherty, Ph.D., Professor of English
Minnesota State University, Mankato

Editors: Shelly Lyons and Jennifer Besel
Designer: Lori Bye
Art Director: Nathan Gassman
Production Specialist: Jane Klenk
The illustrations in this book were created digitally.

Picture Window Books
151 Good Counsel Drive
P.O. Box 669
Mankato, MN 56002-0669
877-845-8392
www.picturewindowbooks.com

Printed in the United States of America in North Mankato, Minnesota.
092009
005618CGS10

All books published by Picture Window Books
are manufactured with paper containing at
least 10 percent post-consumer waste.

Library of Congress Cataloging-in-Publication Data
Meister, Cari.
Everyone feels angry sometimes / by Cari Meister ;
illustrated by Damian Ward.
p. cm. – (Everyone has feelings)
Includes index.
ISBN 978-1-4048-5753-7 (library binding)
ISBN 978-1-4048-6112-1 (paperback)
1. Anger–Juvenile literature. 2. Anger in children–Juvenile literature.
I. Ward, Damian, 1977- II. Title.
BF723.A4M45 2010
152.4'7–dc22   2009024068

Everyone has feelings. Sometimes people feel happy. Other times people feel sad. People can feel angry or scared, too. These feelings are normal.

HAPPY

SAD

ANGRY

SCARED

There are many ways to show anger. There are many ways to feel less angry, too.

Sofie's dog chewed her new shoes.
Sofie feels like her head will explode!

Sofie talks to her mom. They find
a better place to keep her other shoes.

Trevin is building an airplane.
His sister breaks off the wing.

Trevin throws the airplane into the trash can.

Trevin needs time to calm down.
He goes for a run.

Mr. Sanchez keeps a garden.
Mateo bikes over a row of flowers.
Mr. Sanchez yells at Mateo.

Mateo tells Mr. Sanchez he is sorry.
Together they fix the garden.

Isabel wants to be the star in the play.
Her teacher gives the part to Madison.

CLASS PLAY
CASTING TODAY

Isabel's face feels warm. She starts to cry.

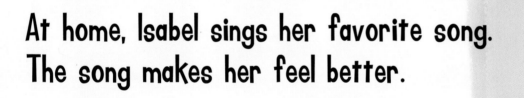

At home, Isabel sings her favorite song.
The song makes her feel better.

Jacob's mom isn't listening to him.
Jacob yells louder and louder.

Jacob's mom tells him he is being rude.
Jacob plays with clay while his mom talks.

Things to do when you feel angry:
- Talk to an adult about your feelings.
- Do 10 jumping jacks or shoot some hoops.
- Sing a song or draw a picture.
- Take three deep breaths.
- Spend some time alone in your room.

Glossary
anger-a feeling like you're mad
explode-to burst suddenly
feelings-emotions; anger, sadness, and happiness are all kinds of feelings.
polite-showing behavior that is respectful toward others

More Books to Read
Bingham, Jane. *Angry*. New York: Crabtree, 2008.
Frost, Helen. *Feeling Angry*. Mankato, Minn.: Pebble Books, 2001.
Medina, Sarah. *Angry*. Chicago: Heinemann Library, 2007.

Internet Sites
FactHound offers a safe, fun way to find Internet sites related to this book.
All of the sites on FactHound have been researched by our staff.
Here's all you do:
Visit *www.facthound.com*
FactHound will fetch the best sites for you!

Look for all of the books in the Everyone Has Feelings series:

Everyone Feels Angry Sometimes

Everyone Feels Happy Sometimes

Everyone Feels Sad Sometimes

Everyone Feels Scared Sometimes